This is 

A book for those kids out there who are struggling to read and write.

Written by Mila Smith & Lindsay Smith

Illustrated by Shannon Kenny & Mila Smith

Second Edition

“This is Mila”, is a true story about a little girl who has challenges to read and write, so instead of focusing on this difference, she channels her energy into her other special and amazing qualities.

She wrote this book for all the kids out there going through the same challenges as her.

For all those who continue to
encourage me to believe in myself.
Thank you.

Mila

This is Mila

Mila loves art.
In fact, she's an
amazing little artist.

Mila loves baking.
She even started her very own baking company called Mila's Munchables.
Her cupcakes are the best!

Mila loves fashion.
She has a very funky sense of style, that everyone compliments her on.

Mila loves to skateboard.
She's getting better and better everyday.
She can even see the Olympics in her future.

Mila has amazing friends;
way more than she can count on both hands.

Mila loves her family
and they really love her.

Mila seems to have it all together,
but she struggles to read and write.

When Mila reads, she sees words differently and when she writes, her letters come out a bit mixed up and sometimes backwards.

This makes her sad and frustrated,
but Mila has a great support system.
Her mom tries her best to help her when
she's struggling and makes sure she knows that
this is just a bump in the road.
This will not hold her back in life.

Mila gets extra help for her reading and writing after school from a special aunty named Nicky. She just loves going to Aunty Nicky because, not only does she get a lot of help, she has a ton of fun!

Mila has met many people who have struggled the same way she does. Some of these people are now doctors, architects, lawyers, artists, designers and Olympians.

Mila knows that it's going to be a long road and she may still get frustrated, but she will keep trying and never give up!

She also wants others going through the same challenges to know, that they are not alone and that they need to focus on all the things that make them so special.

She hopes this book will help them to remember that.

This is Mila

“I may not be there yet,
but I’m closer than
I was yesterday”

-unknown

What are some of the things
that make you special?

This is ________________
(Your Name)

- ____________________
- ____________________
- ____________________
- ____________________
- ____________________
- ____________________
- ____________________
- ____________________
- ____________________
- ____________________

Write down all your talents, accomplishments, hobbies and interests.

YOU ARE AMAZING!
Remember that.

Now think of all the wonderful
things you will accomplish
just by being
YOU!

"I can and I will.
Watch me."

-Carrie Green

Made in the USA
Middletown, DE
08 February 2022

60834625R00015